GENUINE CERTIFIED

CHRISTIAN

IT'S NOT WHAT YOU THINK

ANDY STANLEY

ZONDERVAN.com/
AUTHOR**TRACKER**
follow your favorite authors

ZONDERVAN

Christian Participant's Guide
Copyright © 2012 by North Point Ministries, Inc.

Requests for information should be addressed to:

Zondervan, *Grand Rapids, Michigan 49530*

ISBN 978-0-310-69334-5

Cover and *interior design: Brian Manley (funwithrobots.com)*

Printed in the United States of America

14 15 16 17 18 19 /DCI/ 20 19 18 17 16 15 14 13 12 11 10 9 8 7

CONTENTS

INTRODUCTION

A Problem-Loaded Word
by Andy Stanley

If you and I were in a roomful of randomly chosen people playing a word association game and I called out "Christian," how do you think everyone would respond? What images and adjectives and phrases would be tossed about?

I'm confident our roomful of folks would release a torrent of vastly differing responses—and a good many of their remarks would not be flattering.

The fact is, though it's a word we use all the time, there's no real agreement on what "Christian" actually means.

That's why there are "Christians" on all sides of every political issue, every social issue, every legal issue, every economic issue. It's why nations that are predominantly "Christian" have gone to war with one another.

Mixed-Up Meaning

Christianity sports a seemingly endless array of brands and flavors and traditions. Some would say "Christian" is all about what you believe. Others will argue it's all about how you behave.

Getting personal, some would say they *were* Christians at one time, but no longer are—only to be reproached by those who quickly respond, "No, that's impossible. Once a Christian, always a Christian."

Others would confess they dislike anything associated with the name. They see Christians as judgmental, homophobic moralists who think they're the only ones going to heaven and who secretly relish the fact that everyone else is going to hell—though none of that gets mentioned anywhere in the Bible as a description for Christian.

So "Christian" is whatever you want it to be. You can slap the label on yourself, hang a shiny cross around your neck, and then believe and do just about anything, adopting whatever lifestyle you prefer at the moment. You can hide whoever you are behind it, then easily redefine it whenever you get the urge.

What this boils down to is that none of us knows what "Christian" really represents—since it signifies whatever we choose.

Why is that?

Rare at First

The swirl of confusion over "Christian" is due mainly to the fact that this term is never defined in the New Testament. Jesus didn't refer to his followers in that way, nor did they develop it for themselves.

The word is found three times in the New Testament, but it sprouts up as a label formed by people who were *not* followers of Jesus to designate those who were.

It was a manufactured term with a derogatory slant, meant to be a dig. That's why it's so rare in the Bible. Later, after the New Testament was written, it picked up more traction.

It was somewhat like the buzz years ago that generated "Deadheads" in reference to fans of the band Grateful Dead; at first it was kind of a mocking term, but then they started selling it on T-shirts and the fans loved it and that was that. Over time, the name "Christian" started to stick, and eventually many followers of Jesus would accept it.

But that wasn't the case when the Jesus movement first began.

A Better Word

We'll be exploring another name for Jesus followers that gets far more play in the New Testament. It's got a much narrower scope, and it's far more clearly defined in the Bible—which means it can be somewhat scary for us, as we'll see.

It's a word Jesus often used and also a name embraced by those first-century people who adopted his message for themselves. We'll build on this word and the profound truths and principles that it stands for. We'll also contrast that with what "Christian" has unfortunately represented.

We've often been willing to settle for mere "Christian" instead of pushing for the real thing. But the reality is still calling out for us.

SESSION 1

Brand Recognition

In the book of Acts, we see that people in Antioch (one of the Roman Empire's largest cities) were the first to identify followers of Jesus as "Christians" (11:26).

Later in Acts, when Paul is under arrest and testifying for his defense, he preaches Christ to King Agrippa and expresses his longing for this man to come to faith. The king answers, "Do you think that in such a short time you can persuade me to be a Christian?" (Acts 26:28).

The final occurrence of this word in Scripture is in 1 Peter 4:16. "If you suffer as a Christian," Peter writes, "do not be ashamed, but praise God that you bear that name" (1 Peter 4:16). The implication is that those persecuting the followers of Jesus had thrown this label "Christian" at them, but Peter urges his readers to see the intended slight as cause to praise God.

But the New Testament highlights a different name for the followers of Jesus—and exploring it will both teach and challenge us.

DISCUSSION STARTER

What comes to mind when you think of the word "Christian" (associations, people, etc.)? How would you normally define this term? What has it primarily meant to you in the past?

How have you noticed that other people define this word differently than you do?

VIDEO OVERVIEW

For Session 1 of the DVD

In the book of Acts, we see a Jesus community forming in a city called Antioch (in modern Turkey), where many—both Jews and Gentiles—embraced this new faith.

Church leaders in Jerusalem sent a man named Barnabas to Antioch to observe and help this new church. Barnabas later brought a man named Saul (known later as Paul) there to help him. "For a whole year," we read in Acts 11:26, "Barnabas and Saul met with the church and taught great numbers of people. *The disciples were called Christians first at Antioch.*" So "Christians" was a label that others gave them.

In the New Testament—specifically in the four Gospels and in Acts—a different term is used more consistently to describe these people who were part of this Jesus movement. It's the term "disciple." Notice again Acts 11:26: "The *disciples* were called Christians first at Antioch."

What is a disciple? It simply means a learner, a pupil, an apprentice, an adherent, or a follower.

A disciple looks to a certain other person as the authority and the example for *everything*. A disciple always answers yes to whatever that person asks or requires of him.

That brings us to this uncomfortable question: Are *we* disciples? Or are we just Christians? If we're disciples of Jesus, then no matter what he asks of us, the answer must be yes.

Jesus gave his disciples the bottom line of what it means to be his disciple. On the night before he was crucified, he told them, "A new command I give you: *Love one another.* As I have loved you, so you must love one another" (John 13:33–34). That's how he wanted them to characterize their relationships.

He wanted them to love one another in such a way that outsiders looking on would be drawn to say, "Look how they *love!*" He wanted them to be a community of people defined by unconditional, generous, compassionate love.

Jesus said this was how others would know we're really his followers. Not by how long we pray, how loud we preach, or what we do on Sunday mornings, but how we love one another.

What would it look like *in your world* to love the people around you the way Jesus loves you? By God's grace, just try it.

Trying it won't mean that your life will be free of problems. After all, Jesus was crucified.

This isn't a means to an end; it is what it means to follow Jesus.

VIDEO NOTES

_____

_____

_____

_____

_____

_____

_____

_____

_____

_____

_____

_____

_____

_____

_____

_____

_____

_____

_____

_____

DISCUSSION QUESTIONS

1. What major differences among Christians do you find hard to understand or explain?

2. What does the word "disciple" bring to your mind? What have you learned about the meaning of this word according to the New Testament?

3. In what ways have you looked to Jesus as a model and standard for major decisions in your life?

4. How comfortable are you thinking of yourself as a "disciple"
    of Jesus? Have you ever thought of yourself this way? What
    does being a "disciple" mean to you?

5. Why do you think Jesus puts so much emphasis on love as
    the distinguishing characteristic of his disciples?

6. In general, do you think the followers of Jesus in your com-
    munity think of themselves as "Christians" or "disciples"?
    What difference do you see this making?

MILEPOSTS

- The word "Christian" can mean anything we want it to because it's never clearly defined in Scripture. Originally, it was a derogatory term that outsiders used for followers of Jesus.

- The New Testament emphasizes a different word for those who follow Jesus: *disciples*. It's a disturbing and challenging term because it's so clearly defined.

- Jesus tells his disciples that love for one another is to be our distinguishing characteristic, our defining mark that attracts outsiders to him.

MOVING FORWARD

Are you truly a disciple of Jesus? Or are you settling for just being a Christian? Keep reflecting on the command and calling from Jesus that *love* be your distinguishing characteristic as his follower. Think about it in regard to each of your most important relationships. What will it look like for *love* to be your first priority?

CHANGING YOUR MIND

This session's key Scripture passage is a reminder of the highest calling and the distinguishing characteristic that Jesus has given all who follow him:

A new command I give you: Love one another.
As I have loved you, so you must love one another.
By this everyone will know that you are my disciples,
if you love one another.
John 13:34–35

PREPARATION FOR SESSION 2

To help you prepare for Session 2, use these suggested devotions during the week leading up to your small group meeting.

Day One

Read the words of Jesus in John 13:34–35. Express as fully as possible, in your own words, all that Jesus is teaching here.

Day Two

Turn to the book of 1 John toward the back of the New Testament. Concentrate today on verses 7 and 8 in chapter 4. How do these two verses reinforce what Jesus stated in John 13:34–35?

Day Three

Focus today on 1 John 4:9. Again, in what specific ways does this verse reinforce the words of Jesus in John 13:34–35?

Day Four

Reflect today on 1 John 4:10. As you do, what particular links do you

see with the words of Jesus in John 13:34–35?

Day Five

Concentrate today on 1 John 4:11. Once more, in what specific ways do

you see this verse reinforcing the words of Jesus in John 13:34–35?

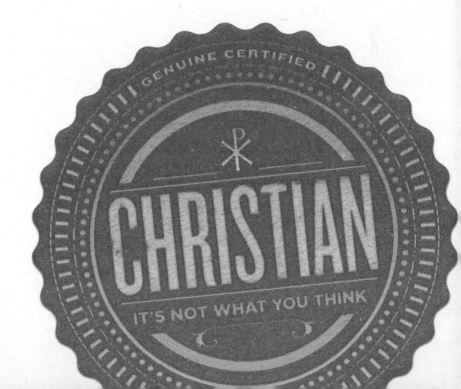

Last Session

We can hide behind the word "Christian" because its meaning isn't specifically taught in the Bible. So "Christians" can pretty much do anything they want and believe anything they want. In the New Testament, however, those who follow Jesus are called something else: disciples. To a very challenging degree for us, the Bible clearly defines this word. Specifically, Jesus calls his disciples *to love one another* as the critical distinctive in their lives.

SESSION 2

Quitters

Anne Rice, one of today's most successful writers, first won fame with her *Vampire Chronicles* in the 1970s. About a decade ago, she spoke of "a new spiritual beginning" as she re-embraced the Christian faith of her childhood and began writing a series of books about the life of Christ. She told the story of her spiritual journey in a book entitled *Called Out of Darkness*.

But in 2010 she announced her decision to "quit being a Christian" and spoke of Christians as being "quarrelsome, hostile, disputatious, and deservedly infamous." She reaffirmed her commitment to Christ, but added, "Following Christ does not mean following his followers. Christ is infinitely more important than Christianity and always will be, no matter what Christianity is, has been, or might become."

Many of us have felt that way. We've experienced being fed up with Christianity. In the midst of life's disappointments, perhaps we've sensed that God hasn't done what we were led to expect him to do. We're torn; we don't want to give up Jesus, but we're unsure we want to continue being associated with anything "Christian."

The apostle John points us to a better way, the way of a disciple.

DISCUSSION STARTER

Have you ever felt tired of Christianity and of trying to live a Christian life? If so, what factors led to that feeling?

Perhaps there are others close to you who have completely turned away from Christianity. What reasons did they express for doing this? How much of it had to do with their views of Jesus himself?

VIDEO OVERVIEW

For Session 2 of the DVD

In his old age, the apostle John wrote a letter to followers of Jesus who had been dispersed throughout the Roman Empire. With the perspective of his long, hard, eventful life, he reiterated the point Jesus had made in John 13: "Dear friends, let us love one another, for love comes from God" (1 John 4:7).

John emphasized that God, in his essence, is love, and that love was proven to us in Jesus: "Whoever does not love does not know God, because God is love. This is how God showed his love among us: he sent his one and only Son into the world that we might live through him. This is love: not that we loved God, but that he loved us and sent his Son as an atoning sacrifice for our sins" (4:8–10).

John could never doubt this love because he had seen it in Jesus, as an eyewitness.

God's love is for everyone. Every single person we encounter is someone God loves—and for that individual, God has sent his Son as an atoning sacrifice. John had personally seen Jesus offered on the cross as this sacrifice. And now, decades later, he was as convinced as ever that Jesus was the Son of God who came to be the sacrifice for our sin.

Because of that, John says, we have an obligation: "Dear friends, since God so loved us, *we also ought to love one another*" (4:11). The little Greek word translated here as "ought" is a financial term about indebtedness. There's a debt-debtor relationship in the gospel that we need to understand. It's there between us and every single person we ever meet, and it's there also between God and us. Since God so loved us, we owe it *to others* to love them. More specifically, since God loves others, we owe it *to God* to love others.

When others are unlovable, we can remember that we're called to love them because God chose first to love *us*.

There's a sense in which we're indebted to God because of

his overwhelming love for us, for which he doesn't even want us to pay him back. He is saying, "In return, all I ask is that you *love other people.*"

We're to love others in such a remarkable way that outsiders will notice.

Our problem is that for too long we've settled for the brand "Christianity" and we've given up our leverage in our culture. We gave it up when we opted for something other than love.

VIDEO NOTES

_____

_____

_____

_____

_____

_____

_____

_____

_____

_____

_____

_____

_____

_____

_____

_____

_____

_____

_____

DISCUSSION QUESTIONS

1. What common characteristics of Christians do you find disturbing? How do they compare with the way Jesus comes across in the New Testament?

2. How convinced are you that God truly loves everyone? Do you see any differences in how he loves people?

3. In your own spiritual journey, how have you grown in experiencing and understanding more of God's love?

4. In what ways have you felt overwhelmed by God's love for you?

5. Who is a person you find difficult to love? Why is loving this person so difficult?

6. What would change most in your community if those who follow Jesus truly loved one another?

MILEPOSTS

- The New Testament further reinforces the point Jesus taught in John 13:34–35—that the main characteristic and defining mark of his followers is *how we love.*

- God, in his essence, *is* love, and his love is for everyone.

- Since God so loved us, we owe it to others to love them. We're in a sense indebted to God for his love for us, and in response he asks us to love others.

MOVING FORWARD

How much attention have you given lately to the love God has shown you, especially through what Jesus has done for you? Are you keeping this in the forefront of your mind and heart? Does your reflection on the life and death of Jesus fill you with an ever-increasing awareness of how great God's love really is? And does it fill you with an ever-increasing awareness of your privilege and obligation to love others? At this moment in your life, let your genuine experience of God's love take you forward into a genuine expansion of your love for others.

CHANGING YOUR MIND

In this session's key passage, the apostle John reinforces the teaching

Jesus gave about the supremacy of love. Let these words fuel your own

lifelong pursuit of love:

> *Dear friends, let us love one another,*
> *for love comes from God. Everyone who loves*
> *has been born of God and knows God.*
> *Whoever does not love does not know God,*
> *because God is love.*
> *1 John 4:7–8*

PREPARATION FOR SESSION 3

To help you prepare for Session 3, use these suggested devotions during the week leading up to your small group meeting.

Day One

Look over the statements and commands Jesus expressed to his disciples in Matthew 28:16–20. How can this passage help us understand the meaning of the word "disciple"?

Day Two

In 1 Corinthians 9:19–23, think about how Paul related to people who weren't already followers of Jesus. What encouragement do you find here for your relationships with people who don't follow Jesus?

Day Three

Return to Paul's example in 1 Corinthians 9:19–23. In your own words, describe Paul's main *goal or purpose* in his relationships with outsiders.

Day Four

Once again, look over 1 Corinthians 9:19–23. Think about the way Paul uses the word "win." How would you define what he means by this term and what it involves?

Day Five

Read 1 Corinthians 5. The particular details of this situation may seem obscure, but what are the main principles that Paul appears to be trying to get across here as it relates to our relationships with people who are *not* followers of Jesus (see especially verses 12 and 13)?

Last Session

The key difference between "Christian" and "disciple" is simply this: "Christian" is often about what a person merely *believes*; "disciple" is all about what a person actually *does*. Because God, in his essence, *is love*—and he loves everyone—we too are called to love others profoundly and unconditionally and indiscriminately. In this way we display a sense of indebtedness to God, who has loved us so completely and overwhelmingly.

SESSION 3
Insiders, Outsiders

People who aren't followers of Jesus and don't consider themselves Christians often expect more of us than we expect of ourselves. They say we don't act like they imagine Jesus would. So there's this tension.

Walter Isaacson, in his biography of Apple founder, Steve Jobs, includes this observation from Jobs: "The juice goes out of Christianity when it becomes too based on faith rather than on living like Jesus or seeing the world as Jesus saw it."

Jesus said that the defining characteristic of those who follow him is how they love one another—not simply what they believe. It's a challenging assignment. When Jesus gave it to us (in John 13:34–35), he was speaking primarily of loving those within the Jesus community.

But how should Jesus followers treat people who *aren't* Jesus followers—those who are outside the faith?

DISCUSSION STARTER

When it comes to Christians judging those who are not Christians, what has been your experience—either as the one judging or the one being judged?

In your own church and perhaps other churches in your community, to what degree have you seen Christians wrongly judging those who are not followers of Jesus?

VIDEO OVERVIEW

For Session 3 of the DVD

At the end of the gospel of Matthew, as the followers of Jesus were gathered on a hillside before he left the earth, Jesus gave them their marching orders: *"Go and make disciples"* (Matthew 28:19). He didn't say, "Go make Christians."

His closest followers obeyed this command and developed Jesus communities. They lived their lives and spoke about Jesus in such a way that others were drawn to him and became his followers as well.

This movement grew dramatically for the first three hundred years. Then the Roman Empire adopted Christianity as its official religion, and things went bad. Now the church had earthly power. They decided not to leverage love anymore, but to leverage other things.

So the marching orders began to sound more like this: "Therefore go and impose Christian teachings, values, and worldview on everyone." That's the message of a group that's in control. But it wasn't the message of Jesus or of the New Testament.

Anytime the church leverages anything other than love, we go backward, not forward, in our influence.

Earlier, Jesus followers had understood that their goal was to win others to the faith. Paul was the ultimate example of this. He wanted to create Jesus followers out of people who had no interest in that—people who had their own religions and ways of life, their own worldviews. And they weren't looking for a new one.

Here was Paul's approach: "Though I am free and belong to no man, I make myself a slave to everyone, to win as many as possible" (1 Corinthians 9:19). He didn't "power up" or become judgmental; rather he made himself the slave of others—in order to win them. Paul said that around Jews, he became like a Jew to win them to Christ. Around Gentiles, he became like a Gentile to win them to Christ. It was all to win as many as possible. Paul knew this was the only way to cause others to become Jesus followers.

We learn more about Paul's approach in 1 Corinthians 5. In addressing a situation of gross sexual immorality by a man who was part of the church at Corinth, Paul stated that while we should *not* divorce ourselves relationally from those who aren't Jesus followers and whose behavior or morality we don't agree with, we *are* to discipline those inside the Jesus community when their lifestyles are inconsistent with the teachings of Jesus. That discipline may include distancing ourselves from them relationally.

We're *not* to judge outsiders; we *are* to judge insiders.

VIDEO NOTES

DISCUSSION QUESTIONS

1. In your community, what expectations do people who aren't
    Jesus followers have of those who are?

2. In what ways do you see Christians trying to leverage any-
    thing other than love to try to influence culture?

3. What are the essential requirements for "winning over"
    someone to a whole new way of thinking or believing?

4. What words and actions and attitudes of Christians cause others to feel threatened or coerced?

5. What are the most common ways that Christians come across as judgmental toward those who are not followers of Jesus?

6. If we have no business holding unbelievers accountable for their behavior, how does this free us in the way we relate to them?

MILEPOSTS

- Whenever the church leverages anything other than love, we go backward, not forward, in our influence among outsiders.

- The only effective way to cause others to become Jesus followers is to *win* them.

- Followers of Jesus, as part of his church, are given moral standards from God to be accountable to. But we must never seek to impose these standards on outsiders. We're to judge *insiders*, never *outsiders*.

MOVING FORWARD

Have you been guilty of judging the actions and behavior of those who aren't followers of Jesus? Do they tend to sense judgment from you instead of love and concern? Do you have a tendency to try to impose your standards on them? Make the decision now to keep others free from any such burden you might want to place on them. Commit yourself to doing whatever it takes to truly *win* them to the love of God.

CHANGING YOUR MIND

In these words, Paul reminds us that our calling to those in our world who are not followers of Jesus is to lovingly *win* them and *not* to judge them.

What business is it of mine to judge those outside the church?
Are you not to judge those inside?
God will judge those outside.
1 Corinthians 5:12–13

PREPARATION FOR SESSION 4

To help you prepare for Session 4, use these suggested devotions during the week leading up to your small group meeting.

Day One

Read Matthew 5:1–5. What do you see as the main points that Jesus is teaching his disciples?

Day Two

Continue reading in Matthew 5 and reflect on verses 6–9. Again, what do you see as the main points Jesus is teaching his followers in these verses?

Day Three

Reflect today on Matthew 5:10–12. As we begin to take these teachings more seriously, what effect is it likely to have?

Day Four

Look today at the word picture Jesus gives in Matthew 5:13. What does he want us to understand most from this?

Day Five

Today, reflect on Matthew 5:14–16 and the word picture Jesus gives there. What is Jesus asking us to do—and how can it actually be accomplished?

Last Session

Loving others represents our marching orders in this world, the calling Jesus gave to all who follow him. As expressed toward other people who are not yet Jesus followers, this love means seeking to *win* them by lovingly serving them. We're *not* to impose the moral standards that Jesus teaches his followers; instead we're to hold one another *within* the Jesus community accountable for those standards.

SESSION 4

Showing Up

How did the movement of Jesus followers spread so quickly and widely in the first few centuries after his death and resurrection? How did that happen?

It didn't happen because the Jesus followers decided to be "Christians." It happened because they took Jesus' words seriously. And, over time, they changed the world.

In the gospel of Matthew, we can read the message that got it all going. This was the beginning of the movement, and it happened early in Jesus' ministry. He was laying the foundation of the movement. It was the beginning of the change. It was a revolutionary, world-changing message.

And three hundred years later, the message of Jesus was everywhere. Nobody was worshiping Jupiter anymore.

So, what about us? Why would we settle for "Christian"—something we can't even define—when Jesus gives us such specific instructions?

DISCUSSION STARTER

In your own community, how have you seen the followers of Jesus as preserving and positive influences? What are some of the significant good deeds that have attracted other people, giving them more reason to think highly of God and of what he is doing in your community?

VIDEO OVERVIEW
For Session 4 of the DVD

In the opening verses of the message Jesus began in Matthew 5, he described his followers as poor, sad, meek, righteous, merciful, pure, peaceful, persecuted, insulted people, waiting for a reward in heaven. His listeners that day must have wondered, *Is that really who we are?*

Jesus then gave his disciples two word pictures. He called them "the salt of the earth" and "the light of the world." *That's who you are,* he was telling them.

Salt is a preservative. Jesus was saying, "You're the world's preservative. Without you, everything rots, and culture stinks."

Jesus also called his followers "the light of the world," like a town or city placed on a hilltop, visible all around, day or night. He was saying, *You've been strategically placed to have a shining influence.* And Jesus said, "Let your light shine before others, that they may see your good deeds and glorify your Father in heaven" (5:16).

Jesus wants us to live in such a way that when people see our good actions, they don't say, "What a nice person," but instead recognize something so extraordinary that they begin to connect the dots and give the credit to God.

Be salt. Be light. Let your lifestyle point the way to Jesus.

Think about your own story. The only reason you're a Christian is that others were salt and light in *your* life, even if they didn't know it.

Salt always preserves; light always shows the way. Salt works even when you can't see it working, and light illumines even when you aren't thinking about it.

No matter where you are in your daily life, Jesus has you there as the salt and the light of that world.

So let's not settle for "Christian." Let's ask God how to make us more effective salt and more effective light.

And as God answers that prayer, who knows what he might do in our families, in our communities, in our nation, and in the whole world?

VIDEO NOTES

_____

_____

_____

_____

_____

_____

_____

_____

_____

_____

_____

_____

_____

_____

_____

_____

_____

_____

_____

_____

_____

_____

_____

DISCUSSION QUESTIONS

1. The first Christians embraced the words of Jesus with utter seriousness and ended up changing the world. How much potential for the same kind of change do you see in our world today?

2. What positive influences have followers of Jesus had on our culture in the past or present?

3. In what ways do you wish the followers of Jesus had a stronger influence on our culture?

4. How do followers of Jesus view our world differently than other people? What tension does this create?

5. If followers of Jesus were "salt" and "light" in our world, how could that help to overcome the differences between them and those who don't follow Jesus?

6. What convinces you that all human beings have great worth to God?

MILEPOSTS

- Jesus described his followers with two distinctive word pictures: "the salt of the earth" and "the light of the world." *Wherever you are*, Jesus has you there to be this kind of influence.

- Salt is a preservative. Without the proper influence of Jesus followers, the world's culture will decay.

- Light shows the way. Jesus calls his followers to have such a shining influence through our good deeds that it causes others to give credit to God.

MOVING FORWARD

What does being a "light" in this world mean to you personally? How has God equipped you and prepared you for this? Which areas of darkness do you believe he wants you to shine his light in?

CHANGING YOUR MIND

In these words, Jesus leads us forward into our shining influence in

this world, an influence that shows others the way and draws them

to him:

Let your light shine before others,
that they may see your good deeds
and glorify your Father in heaven.
Matthew 5:16

PREPARATION FOR SESSION 5

To help you prepare for Session 5, use these suggested devotions during the week leading up to your small group meeting.

Day One

In the first chapter of the gospel of John, reflect on the teaching about Jesus ("the Word") in verses 14, 16, and 17. If you had never heard of Jesus, what would you learn about him from these verses? What further questions would you have?

Day Two

Look over the interesting encounter Jesus had with a Samaritan woman in John 4:1–45. What evidence do you see here that Jesus was "full of grace and truth," as expressed in John 1:14?

Day Three

Move today in your reading to John 8:1–11, where Jesus encounters another woman. Again, what evidence do you find here that Jesus was "full of grace and truth"?

Day Four

Reflect today on what happens in the life of Jesus in Mark 2:13–17. As Jesus relates to Levi (also known as Matthew) and his friends, what further evidence do you find that Jesus was "full of grace and truth"?

Day Five

Search again for evidence that Jesus was "full of grace and truth," this time by reading about the day of Jesus' crucifixion in Matthew 23:32–43. What do we learn from the way Jesus related to the two criminals being executed on both sides of him?

GENUINE CERTIFIED

CHRISTIAN

IT'S NOT WHAT YOU THINK

Last Session

The Jesus movement spread rapidly in the first few centuries because the followers of Jesus embraced their calling to be "the salt of the earth" and "the light of the world." They represented a godly preservative. And their lights, displayed in good deeds, showed the way to God, so that others were drawn to become Jesus followers.

SESSION 5

When Gracie Met Truthy

We all think we know something about love—and all of us have experienced love to some extent.

But Jesus tells us to love one another the way *he* loved us.

When we look at how Jesus loved, it's a bit terrifying. We discover that it was messy, and sometimes it seemed inconsistent. At times he seems to be forgiving; at other times he seems to hold everyone accountable. Occasionally he's harsh; in many other moments he's kind. Sometimes he points out sin; on other occasions he seems to ignore it.

Whenever we open the Scriptures and take seriously the teachings of Jesus, there's a tension. We dare not walk away from this tension, even though it's messy and sometimes seems confusing. If we try to resolve it, however, we will give up something very important.

DISCUSSION STARTER

As you've read or heard about the way Jesus treated individuals, what has most surprised or puzzled you?

VIDEO OVERVIEW

For Session 5 of the DVD

In his gospel, John wrote that Jesus, as the Word, "made his dwelling among us," and that he "came from the Father, *full of grace and truth*" (John 1:14). Full to the brim with grace and truth—there's the tension.

We think we know what *grace* is and what *truth* is. Truth says, "Hey, you're accountable." Grace says, "Oh, you're forgiven." Grace says, "You're fine." Truth says, "No, you're broken." Grace says, "It's going to be okay." Truth says, "Oh, you're going to have to work on it."

But John says that Jesus was absolutely full of *both* grace and truth. To further emphasize this, John adds, "grace and truth came through Jesus Christ" (1:17). Grace and truth showed up as a full package in the person of Jesus—*not* a balance between the two, but the full measure of both and the embodiment of both.

This is what made the love of Jesus so messy, so confusing to us at times, and so unpredictable. Jesus was *all* of both grace and truth, and he brought all of it to bear on everyone he talked to and into every situation he encountered.

If we want to know what Jesus meant when he said to love one another, we can watch how Jesus loved. He loved us by calling sin "sin"—and then he paid for it. And having paid for it, he declared, *I don't condemn you.*

We can't let go of truth. God is constantly saying, "Here's what is true; here's how you've got to live; here's how you've got to treat people; here's what you have to do with your morality and your ethics; and here's why you have to be accountable. Sin is destructive, and I don't want it to get you."

We can't let go of grace either, because to some extent sin already has us, and grace is our only way back home. Grace is the only way we'll know that we've connected or reconnected with our heavenly Father.

We need truth, and we need grace.

If Jesus is the embodiment of grace and truth, and if the church is his body—then we are the best expressions of Jesus others will ever know. So we have to be comfortable with the mess and the unfairness and the inconsistency and all the stuff that goes along with managing and hanging on to the tension around grace and truth.

The church is at its best when it embraces grace and truth and refuses to let go of either. The church is to be the dispenser of both.

VIDEO NOTES

DISCUSSION QUESTIONS

1. When you read the Bible (or hear it taught) and experience tension in your understanding of Jesus and how he lives and loves, is that tension something you try to resolve or are you comfortable with it?

2. What's your understanding of the word "grace" and what it represents—both as coming from God and as conveyed by us to other people?

3. What's your understanding of the word "truth" and what it represents—both as coming from God and as conveyed by us to other people?

4. What are the ways you recognize or experience tension between grace and truth? In which direction do you tend to lean?

5. In what ways have you experienced both grace and truth?

6. Why is a "balance" between grace and truth the wrong way to think of what's being taught in this session? What is a better way to think of the relationship between grace and truth?

MILEPOSTS

- When examining how Jesus loved, we find unpredictability and apparent inconsistencies. If we try to resolve this tension, we lose.

- In all his encounters with people, Jesus was always the full embodiment of *both* grace and truth. We, however, tend to see these two in tension.

- We must never let go of either truth or grace; we need *both*. The church is at its best when it embraces both and dispenses both.

MOVING FORWARD

Think about your own commitment and intention to extend to others both truth and grace in full measure. What does that actually mean to you? What will it require from you? We recommend that you make it your goal to reflect deeply on the full manifestation of both grace and truth in the life of Jesus. As you continue reading about him in the New Testament, try to embrace whatever tension arises as you see the love of Jesus in action and as you seek to put it into practice in your relationships.

CHANGING YOUR MIND

These profound words reflect the reason for the tension we often encounter as we observe the surprising and unpredictable ways in which Jesus loved people.

The Word became flesh
and made his dwelling among us.
We have seen his glory,
the glory of the one and only Son,
who came from the Father,
full of grace and truth.
John 1:14

PREPARATION FOR SESSION 6

To help you prepare for Session 6, use these suggested devotions during the week leading up to your small group meeting.

Day One

Focus this week on the brief stories (parables) that Jesus told in Luke 15. What is especially important to note in the background for these stories as indicated in 15:1–3?

Day Two

In the story Jesus told in Luke 15:4–7, what stands out to you? What do you relate to the most in this little story? What do you enjoy the most?

Day Three

In the story Jesus told in Luke 15:8–10, what stands out most to you? What do you relate to most in this story? What do you enjoy most?

Day Four

In the final story in Luke 15 (in Luke 15: 11–32), what do you see as Jesus' main points? What would the audience that day be most surprised to hear in this story?

Day Five

What do you see as the strongest ways in which the three stories in Luke 15 link together?

LAST SESSION

Jesus came to this earth as one who was absolutely *"full* of grace and truth" (John 1:14). In his encounters with people, this worked itself out in surprising and perplexing ways, as he always brought *all* his grace and *all* his truth to bear in every situation. Trying to understand his way of loving can cause tension in us, but it's a healthy tension. We, too, need to hold on fully to both grace and truth in all of our relationships.

SESSION 6

Angry Birds

We've seen in the gospel of John that in Jesus we have the full embodiment of grace and truth. And we go on in the New Testament to discover that as Jesus followers, we also must somehow get to that full embodiment of both grace and truth. If we're just *grace*, or if we're just *truth*, there will always be something missing.

In many scenarios from Jesus' life, we can see how he applied this. He surprises us with his amazing ability to dispense grace and truth in just the right amounts.

So how do we do that as well?

In our last session, we looked at how Jesus modeled the embodiment of grace and truth. In this session, we'll see where he actually taught this. And what made his teaching so significant on this occasion was his audience. It's an audience in which we're sure to find ourselves.

DISCUSSION STARTER

What is the most valuable thing you've ever lost? How did you respond to losing it? Did you eventually find it? If so, how did you react to finding it?

VIDEO OVERVIEW

For Session 6 of the DVD

As Luke 15 begins, Jesus finds himself surrounded by two very different groups. One group, "tax collectors and sinners," felt they were so alienated from God that he would never approve of them.

The other group, "Pharisees and the teachers of the law," believed they were so good that God already approved of them. And they were muttering this about Jesus: "This man welcomes sinners and eats with them."

In response, Jesus told a simple story of a man with a hundred sheep who loses one. Jesus asked his audience, "Doesn't he leave the ninety-nine in the open country and go after the lost sheep until he finds it?" (15:4). Jesus described this man's joy upon finding his lost sheep. "In the same way," Jesus added, "there will be more rejoicing in heaven over one sinner who repents than over ninety-nine righteous persons who do not need to repent" (15:7).

He then told another story of a woman who lost a valuable coin. Again Jesus asked, "Doesn't she light a lamp, sweep the house and search carefully until she finds it?" (15:8). Finding it, the woman was filled with joy. "In the same way," Jesus added, "there is rejoicing in the presence of the angels of God over one sinner who repents" (Luke 15:10).

Jesus then launched a third story; it was about a man with two sons. The older son was a "behaver"; the younger was a "misbehaver." Shockingly, the younger son spurned his relationship with his father and asked for his inheritance. He traveled to a distant country and squandered his new wealth on reckless living—another detail that would shock Jesus' hearers. Having lost everything, the disgraced young man was further battered when a famine struck the land. The only work he could find was feeding pigs with food that he himself began craving. *Surely he was only getting what he deserved.*

But Jesus went on to tell of this starving son coming to his senses and deciding to return home to confess, "Father, I have sinned against heaven and against you. I am no longer worthy to be called your son; make me like one of your hired servants" (15:18–19). *Surely servanthood for life was a worthy fate for this reprobate.*

But Jesus then painted a picture of a stunningly incredible reception for this boy. His father lavished compassion, tenderness, and restoration upon this son who had humiliated him. He called for a celebration feast.

But all this angered the firstborn son. He was angered in the way some Christians are today—Christians who self-righteously believe they deserve better treatment from God than they're getting, and who despise the grace God shows to the "undeserving."

VIDEO NOTES

_____

_____

_____

_____

_____

_____

_____

_____

_____

_____

_____

_____

_____

_____

_____

_____

_____

_____

_____

DISCUSSION QUESTIONS

1. In what ways do you sense alienation from God among peo-
    ple in your community?

2. In what ways do you see evidence of self-righteousness
    among religious people in your community?

3. Are you convinced there's nothing you can do to cause God
    to love you more than he already does? Why or why not?

4. Are you convinced there's nothing *others* can do to cause God to love them more than he already does? Why or why not?

5. In what ways are you tempted to grow slack in your understanding and acceptance of God's *grace*?

6. In what ways are you tempted to grow slack in your understanding and acceptance of God's *truth*?

MILEPOSTS

- We're called to capture and reflect the full embodiment of grace and truth that Jesus manifested in all his encounters with people.

- God seeks out the lost, and he wholeheartedly celebrates their return to him. In this same way, we're to have our hearts saturated with his love toward others.

- God wants us to become increasingly more comfortable with embracing the tension between God's grace and God's truth, refusing to let go of either.

MOVING FORWARD

Examine your heart. Do you realize God cannot love you more than he already does? That there's nothing you can do to cause him to love you any more or any less? Do you realize the same is true about God's love for others? Let this saturate your thinking, so that sin (yours and others') will always break your heart ... while repentance will always stir up your highest joy.

CHANGING YOUR MIND

In this concluding statement to one of the brief stories Jesus told, he points us to the joy we can share in as we share his heart toward others:

I tell you, there is rejoicing
in the presence of the angels of God
over one sinner who repents.
Luke 15:10

PREPARATION FOR SESSION 7

To help you prepare for Session 7, use these suggested devotions during the week leading up to your small group meeting.

Day One

Look at the encounter Jesus had with certain religious leaders in Matthew 15:1–9. What exactly were these men doing wrong? In this situation, how did Jesus demonstrate his values and his heart and mind?

Day Two

Turn to Romans 13:8. What do you see personally as the right way of understanding the obligation Paul mentions in this verse?

Day Three

Look today at Romans 13:9. What particular significance for your life do you find in Paul's words here?

Day Four

Move today to Romans 13:10. How would you express in your own words what Paul is saying here?

Day Five

Look at the conversation Jesus had in Mark 12:28–34. How does the teaching of Jesus here relate to what you observed in Romans 13:8–10? And how does it relate to the words of Jesus we focused on earlier in John 13:34–35?

LAST SESSION

We see God's grace and truth in overwhelming richness in some stories Jesus told (Luke 15) to a mixed audience of self-aware sinners and self-righteous religious leaders. These stories confirm that God cannot love us more than he already does; there's nothing we can do to cause him to love us more or less. The same is true of his love for others. That's why our hearts should break when others fall into sin, and their repentance and return to God should fill us with overwhelming joy.

SESSION 7

Loopholes

We all like loopholes. They're our way of getting around rules or laws.

Looking for them comes naturally; nobody has to teach us. We're always searching for them.

Christians love loopholes, as all religious people do. Every religion has a book or a list, and every religion has theologians to help people get around actually doing the stuff written in those books or those lists. Religion gives you a belief system that you don't really follow; when it gets really difficult, you find a loophole.

Loophole Christians really love theology. Theology is where we build the barricades that keep us from having to do what the Bible actually says. All kinds of horrible things have happened in the name of theology.

But the truth is, when you're a follower of Jesus, you quit searching for loopholes. And you start looking for something else. You start asking a completely different set of questions.

In a conversation Jesus had with some experts on loopholes, we discover something that should make us rethink our whole approach to Christianity as it relates to these things.

DISCUSSION STARTER

What are some of the loopholes you've seen other people come up with and take advantage of? Did their reasoning behind this strike you as clever, humorous, aggravating—or something else?

And how about you? What loopholes have you found yourself looking for and making use of?

VIDEO OVERVIEW

For Session 7 of the DVD

Jesus doesn't like it when we use his Father's words to avoid doing his Father's will.

We all do this when we ignore the truths in the Bible we find inconvenient. We make lists, but our lists never fully match the lists in the Bible. We pick and choose.

Jesus pushed back against this. He takes us back to what God first had in mind when he gave his commandments in Scripture.

This was in his thinking as he told his disciples: "A new command I give you: Love one another" (John 13:34). He knew God wanted this to be primary. Then Jesus added, "As I have loved you, so you must love one another."

More than twenty years later, Paul echoed this as he wrote to the Jesus followers in Rome: "Let no debt remain outstanding, except the continuing debt to love one another, for whoever loves others has fulfilled the law" (Romans 13:8). In other words, we should pay our debts—but this debt of loving one another is one we can never pay off. We owe it to the people around us to love them, because we owe it to our heavenly Father in light of how much he loves us.

Paul went on to say that all the commands in the Old Testament "are summed up in this one command: 'Love your neighbor as yourself'" (13:9).

This is what Jesus taught as well. The religious leaders asked him, "What's the greatest command?" He responded, "Love the Lord your God with all your heart and with all your soul and with all your mind and with all your strength." Then he added, "The second is this: 'Love your neighbor as yourself.' There is no commandment greater than these" (Mark 12:30–31). He was saying that *everything* else is secondary.

Loving God and loving your neighbor as yourself—this is the filter through which we're to make every decision. The rest of Scripture is simply commentary on how to love in this way.

Disciples of Jesus use the Scriptures as a mirror. Each day they ask, "What does love require of me?" Not simply, "What does the Bible say?"

Living and loving this way is much harder and more complicated than being a loophole Christian. We reach out toward people we don't like, because that's what Jesus did. This can lead us into uncomfortable places and new kinds of relationships.

This approach has nothing to do with abandoning your faith or compromising. It has everything to do with looking at others and asking yourself, "What does love require of me?"

VIDEO NOTES

_____

_____

_____

_____

_____

_____

_____

_____

_____

_____

_____

_____

_____

_____

_____

_____

_____

_____

DISCUSSION QUESTIONS

1. Why are we so eager to find loopholes—especially religious loopholes?

2. How do Christians manufacture extra rules in order to preserve their own comforts or biases?

3. How would you describe your view of theology? Do you see theology as helpful or harmful?

4. How can you tell if you're more in love with the commands in the Bible than with the *Commander*?

5. Are you convinced that Jesus understood his Father's intentions as written in the Bible? Why or why not?

6. How would you answer the question, "What does love require of me?"

MILEPOSTS

- We naturally love loopholes as a way of escaping God's requirements that we find uncomfortable, and we base these loopholes on the Bible.

- But Jesus doesn't like it when we use his Father's words to avoid doing his Father's will.

- Loving God and loving others is to be our filter for rightly guiding every situation in life. We're to always ask, "What does love require of me?"

MOVING FORWARD

What does it mean practically for you to be a debtor to other people, to owe them the continuing debt of love, according to Romans 13:8? Is this a new way of thinking for you? What will help you remember this obligation toward others in your daily life?

CHANGING YOUR MIND

Let these words from Paul remind you of how strongly we owe it to God and to others to extend love to everyone:

Let no debt remain outstanding,
except the continuing debt to love one another,
for whoever loves others has fulfilled the law.
Romans 13:8

PREPARATION FOR SESSION 8

To help you prepare for Session 8, use these suggested devotions during the week leading up to your small group meeting.

Day One

Turn today to Matthew 22:37–40, which is another account of a passage we looked at last week (Mark 12:28–34). Notice especially verse 40. What do you find most significant in this verse? What do you think Jesus wants us to understand most from his words here?

Day Two

To help review and reinforce where we've been in these sessions, look at Acts 11:26. What new understanding do you have of this passage?

Day Three

Look today at Acts 26:28 and 1 Peter 4:16. Together with yesterday's verse, these passages represent the three places the word "Christian" is used in the Bible. Taken together, what do they tell us about this word?

Day Four

Today, reflect on the way the word "disciple" is used in Acts 6:7, 9:26, and 9:36. What new understanding do you have of this word?

Day Five

Finally, turn once more to the crucial statement in John 13:34–35. What new understanding do you have of these profound words of Jesus?

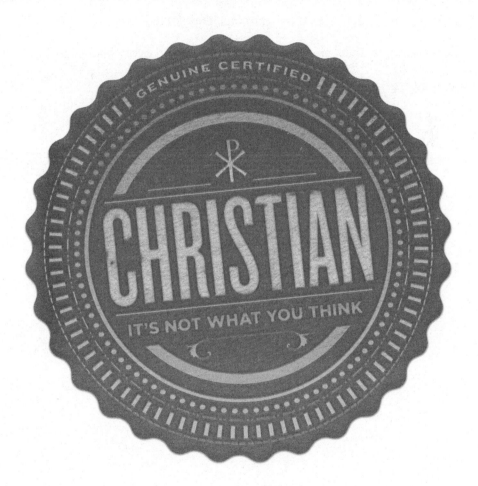

GENUINE CERTIFIED

CHRISTIAN

IT'S NOT WHAT YOU THINK

LAST SESSION

We all love loopholes, especially religious loopholes that we attach to some Scripture passage, allowing us to appear more obedient to God than we really are. But disciples of Jesus do not look for such loopholes. They recognize the higher challenge of the *love* their Lord calls them to as their greatest pursuit. Each day, in every aspect of life, they learn to ask, "What does love require of me?"

SESSION 8

Working It Out

One day some people came to Jesus with a trick question. They wanted him to tell them which was the greatest of all the hundreds of Old Testament commands.

"Jesus quickly answered, 'Love the Lord your God with all your heart and with all your soul and with all your mind.' This is the first and greatest commandment. And the second is like it: 'Love your neighbor as yourself'" (Matthew 22:37–39).

Somewhere along the way, the followers of Jesus have lost sight of what Jesus said next: "All the Law and the Prophets hang on these two commandments" (22:40).

This means that every time we pick up our Bibles for guidance, every time we teach a lesson from it, every time we search its pages to discover what we should do in a particular situation, every time we ask, "What does the Bible say about this?" we're to make sure we look at it through the filter of loving God with all our hearts, souls, and minds, and loving our neighbors as ourselves.

DISCUSSION STARTER

Think of the people who have had the most significant influence in your life, for better or worse. How did they profoundly love you or hurt you?

VIDEO OVERVIEW

For Session 8 of the DVD

There are two categories of people that have influenced our lives profoundly: *those who have hurt us and those who have loved us.* And their impact was *not* because of what they believed; rather, it was something we felt and experienced that spoke directly to our souls.

This is why it's so extraordinarily important that Jesus followers understand his message about the priority of loving others. Love is our greatest opportunity.

If we want to see people change, if we want to influence their futures, we're to love them profoundly.

You can take this to the next level by engaging with these three statements:

1.   Don't do anything that will hurt *you.*

2. Don't do anything that will hurt *someone else.*

3. Don't be *mastered* by anything.

These are three handles that help us in learning to treat people in ways that heal their hurts and love them toward our Savior, who loved them so much that he died for them.

Love requires that you not do anything that hurts *you,* because your heavenly Father loves you as his child and in hurting yourself, you hurt him.

Love requires that you never make a moral decision, a sexual decision, an ethical decision, a relational decision, or a professional decision that hurts you, because when you hurt yourself, you hurt the One and the ones who love you most.

Love also requires that you do nothing to hurt *anyone else* in your interpersonal relationships, because every person you encounter is someone your heavenly Father sent his Son to die for—even your worst enemies, even the people who can't stand you.

Love also requires that you not be *mastered* by anything. Whenever you're mastered by something, it keeps you from loving. No one should have to compete with your alcohol or your porn or your prescription drug addiction or your anger or with anything that masters you. Refuse to be mastered by anything, because God is your Master. Love requires that you get rid of *anything* in your life that competes with his lordship.

In the beginning of the Jesus movement, with the simple idea to love one another, Jesus followers were able to influence their culture so profoundly that a form of paganism we can't even imagine was turned upside down and disappeared.

If that commitment to love again characterizes our lives and our churches, we'll have leverage in our culture beyond comprehension. But when we abandon love as our point of leverage, we continue to lose leverage. We can't preach people into loving Jesus or loving one another. We can't preach people out of destructive habits and addictions. These transformations happen only when our love is so attractive that it's irresistible.

VIDEO NOTES

_____

_____

_____

_____

_____

_____

_____

_____

_____

_____

_____

_____

_____

_____

_____

_____

_____

_____

_____

_____

_____

_____

DISCUSSION QUESTIONS

1. How central is *love for God* and *love for others* to your understanding of the Bible's message?

2. How central is *love for God* and *love for others* to the moral and ethical standards you apply to your life?

3. How have you already grown in understanding what love requires? How have your attitudes changed over time?

4.   What part do our beliefs play in the influence we have on other people?

5.   What challenges are you likely to encounter if you truly seek to avoid hurting yourself, hurting others, and being mastered by anything?

MILEPOSTS

- The people who have influenced our lives most profoundly are those who have either significantly hurt us or significantly loved us. Their influence was not because of their beliefs.

- If we want to influence people and see transformation in their lives, we must love them profoundly.

- We must (1) do nothing that hurts us, (2) do nothing that hurts others, and (3) not be mastered by anything.

MOVING FORWARD

Step back and consider your overall approach to decisions, relationships, activities, and responsibilities. As you grow in viewing *all* of these through the "filter" of loving God and loving others—what difference will it make? What expectations do you have? If it leads to difficulties, tension, and hardship, will you be ready and willing to keep pressing forward in this direction?

CHANGING YOUR MIND

In this passage, Jesus answered a questioner by quoting from the Old Testament and showing again the supremacy of love.

> *"Love the Lord your God with all your heart*
> *and with all your soul and with all your mind."*
> *This is the first and greatest commandment.*
> *And the second is like it: "Love your neighbor*
> *as yourself." All the Law and the Prophets*
> *hang on these two commandments.*
> *Matthew 22:37–40*

Leader's Guide

So, You're the Leader...

Is that intimidating? Perhaps exciting? You probably have a mental picture of what it will look like to lead—what you'll say and how group members will respond. Before you get too far into planning, there are some things you should know about leading a small group discussion.

Basics About Leading

Cultivate discussion — It's easy to assume that a group meeting lives or dies based on the quality of your ideas. That's not true. It's the ideas of everyone in the group that make a small group meeting successful. Your role is to create an environment in which people feel safe to share their thoughts. That's how relationships will grow and thrive among your group members.

Here's a basic truth about spiritual growth within the context of community: the study materials aren't as important as the relationships through which those materials take practical shape in the lives of the group members. The more meaningful the relationships, the more meaningful the study will be. The best materials in the world won't change lives in a sterile environment.

Point to the material — A good host or hostess creates an environment where people can connect relationally. He or she knows when to help guests connect and when to stay out of the way when those connections are happening organically. As a small group leader, sometimes you'll simply read a discussion question and invite everyone to respond. The conversation will take care of itself. At other times, you may need to encourage group members to share their ideas. Remember, some of the best insights will come from the people in your group. Go with the flow, but be ready to nudge the conversation in the right direction when necessary.

Depart from the material — We've carefully designed this study for your small group. We've written the materials and designed the questions to elicit the kinds of conversations we think will be most helpful to your group members. That doesn't mean you should stick rigidly to the materials. Knowing when to depart from them is more art than science, but no one knows more about your group than you do.

The stories, questions, and exercises are here to provide a framework for exploration. But different groups have different chemistries and different motivations. Sometimes the best way to start a small group discussion is to ask, "Does anyone have a personal insight you'd like to share from this week's material?" Then sit back and listen.

Stay on track — This is the flip side to the previous point. There's an art to facilitating an engaging conversation. While you want to leave space for group members to think through the discussion, you also need to keep your objectives in mind. Make sure the discussion is contributing to the bottom line for the week. Don't let the discussion veer off into tangents. Interject politely in order to refocus the group.

Pray — This is the most important thing you can do as a leader. The best leaders get out of God's way and let him communicate through them. Remember: books don't teach God's Word; neither do sermons or discussion groups. God speaks into the hearts of men and women. Prayer is a vital part of communicating with him.

Pray for your group members. Pray for your own leadership. Pray that God is not only present at your group meetings, but is directing them.

We hope you find these suggestions helpful. And we hope you enjoy leading this study. You will find additional guidelines and suggestions for each session in the Leader's Guide notes that follow.

Leader's Guide
Session Notes

Session 1 — Brand Recongnition

Bottom Line

We have a higher and better calling than simply being "Christians." Jesus calls us to be his "disciples"—which means we're constantly learning from him, submitting to him, and constantly displaying the distinguishing mark of genuine love for others.

Discussion Starter

Use the "Discussion Starter" printed in Session 1 of the Participant's Guide to "break the ice"—and to help everyone see the inadequacy of the term "Christian."

Notes for Discussion Questions

1. **What major differences among Christians do you find hard to understand or explain?**

    Allow each person in the group to articulate this as fully as possible.

2.   **What does the word "disciple" bring to your mind? What have you learned about the meaning of this word according to the New Testament?**

Help direct the discussion to the meaning of disciple as given in the DVD teaching content, but also welcome other observations from the group members.

3.   **In what ways have you looked to Jesus as a model and standard for major decisions in your life?**

Share your honest response here—which will be the best encouragement for thorough, honest answers from the rest of the group.

4.   **How comfortable are you thinking of yourself as a "disciple" of Jesus? Have you ever thought of yourself this way? What does being a "disciple" mean to you?**

Again, your genuine response will help open up everyone else in the group to share candidly.

5.   **Why do you think Jesus puts so much emphasis on love as the distinguishing characteristic of his disciples?**

You may want to broaden the discussion by directing attention to such passages as 1 John 4:7–8; 1 Peter 1:22; 1 John 1:5; 2 Corinthians 13:11; Ephesians 2:4; John 3:16; Exodus 34:6; Psalm 86:5, 15; and Deuteronomy 30:6.

6.   **In general, do you think the followers of Jesus in your community think of themselves as "Christians" or "disciples"? What difference do you see this making?**

Help direct the discussion to the distinctions between these two terms as given in the DVD teaching content, but also welcome other observations from the group members. As you close the discussion for this session, ask each person in the group to pray a sentence prayer that acknowledges God's love for us.

Moving Forward

The goal here is to help everyone in the group begin to build the habit and the mindset of becoming a genuine disciple of Jesus, marked by a lifestyle of love.

Preparation for Session 2

Remember to point out the brief daily devotions that the group members can complete and which will help greatly in stimulating discussion in your next session. These devotions will enable everyone to dig into the Bible and start wrestling with the topics that will come up next time.

Session 2 — Quitters

Bottom Line

Throughout the New Testament we see the Lord's emphasis on love as the distinguishing mark of true disciples, true followers of Jesus. It's a love that flows freely from the God of love and from the love he freely pours out on us through his Son, Jesus, and his sacrifice for our sins.

Discussion Starter

Use the "Discussion Starter" printed in Session 2 of the Participant's Guide to "break the ice"—and to help everyone see that the system of "Christianity" is no replacement for a genuine experience of the living Jesus.

Notes for Discussion Questions

1. **What common characteristics of Christians do you find disturbing? How do they compare with the way Jesus comes across in the New Testament?**

    Let your honest answer lead the way for others.

2.   **How convinced are you that God truly loves everyone? Do you see any difference in how he loves people?**

This could be an opportune moment to bring in the amazing reach of the gospel—extending to "the whole world" (1 John 2:2).

3.   **In your own spiritual journey, how have you grown in experiencing and understanding more of God's love?**

Again, your genuine response will help open up everyone else in the group to share candidly.

4.   **In what ways have you felt overwhelmed by God's love for you?**

Again, your genuine response will help open up everyone else in the group to share candidly. When you think of the fact that God sees—clearly and immediately—every instance of our irresponsibility, how do you react?

5.   **Who is a person you find difficult to love? Why is loving this person so difficult?**

Most of us need lots of help in becoming more honest with ourselves, so allow plenty of time for discussion.

6.   **What would change most in your community if those who follow Jesus truly loved one another?**

Encourage a strong desire to be part of God's mission in reaching nonbelievers in your community. As you close the discussion for this session, ask each person in the group to pray a sentence prayer asking for God's active work in bringing people in your community into a relationship with himself through the power of the gospel.

Moving Forward

The goal here is to help group members give plenty of thought about the love of God, so that it compels them to share this love with others.

Preparation for Session 3

Remember to point out the brief daily devotions that the group members can complete and that will help greatly in stimulating discussion in your next session. These devotions will enable everyone to dig into the Bible and start wrestling with the topics that will come up next time.

Session 3 — Insiders, Outsiders

Bottom Line

We have no business holding non-Jesus followers accountable for their behavior. For those who have never "signed on" to the teachings of Jesus about marriage, finances, integrity, and so forth, we have no business trying to impose on them our standards as Jesus followers. *Within* the church, however, we *are* to hold one another accountable for what Jesus teaches. Yet we so often get this backwards. The church is notorious for trying to police the behavior of people outside the church, while doing a poor job policing the behavior of people inside the church.

Discussion Starter

Use the "Discussion Starter" printed in Session 3 of the Participant's Guide to "break the ice"—and to help everyone recognize the tragic mistake of trying to impose Christian standards on those who are not yet won to the gospel.

Notes for Discussion Questions

1.   **In your community, what expectations do people who aren't Jesus followers have of those who are?**

Encourage the kind of sensitivity that will help everyone in your group to be better prepared for opportunities to share the gospel and the love of Jesus with nonbelievers in your community.

2. **In what ways do you see Christians trying to leverage anything other than love to try to influence culture?**
Look for general patterns, rather than naming names.

3. **What are the essential requirements for "winning over" someone to a whole new way of thinking or believing?**
Again, encourage the openness and warmheartedness that will help further the gospel's impact in your community.

4. **What words and actions and attitudes of Christians cause others to feel threatened or coerced?**
Help direct the discussion toward the kind of wrongful judging that is discussed in the DVD teaching content for this session.

5. **What are the most common ways that Christians come across as judgmental toward those who are not followers of Jesus?**

This is more difficult for some people than for others. For those who find it hardest, be careful to avoid making them feel discouraged about this.

6. **If we have no business holding unbelievers accountable for their behavior, how does this free us in the way we relate to them?**

   Encourage the positive realization of what loving others is all about. As you close, ask each person in the group to pray a sentence prayer that recognizes our dependence on God and his grace and truth.

Moving Forward

The goal here is to help everyone in the group to fully recognize the tragic mistake of trying to impose Christian standards on people in the world and to instead make a firm commitment to truly *winning* others to Christ through love.

Preparation for Session 4

Remember to point out the brief daily devotions that the group members can complete and which will help greatly in stimulating discussion in your next session. These devotions will enable everyone to dig into the Bible and start wrestling with the topics that will come up next time.

Session 4 — Showing Up

Bottom Line

Jesus gives us our identity and calling as the salt of the earth and the light of the world. It's our privilege and obligation to be godly influences in the world through our loving acts of service. We're to live in such an extraordinary way that people are drawn to Jesus, the source of life.

Discussion Starter

Use the "Discussion Starter" printed in Session 4 of the Participant's Guide to "break the ice"—and to help everyone see the exalted privilege of being an influence for Christ in our culture.

Notes for Discussion Questions

1. **The first Christians embraced the words of Jesus with utter seriousness and ended up changing the world. How much potential for the same kind of change do you see in our world today?**

    Encourage a strong faith to trust God for his active working in your community and our world through the gospel—a faith that actively prays and seeks opportunities to share the gospel.

2.   **What positive influences have followers of Jesus had on our culture in the past or present?**

This could promote gratefulness to God for how he has faithfully empowered believers as his witnesses in the past—and how he still does this today.

3.   **In what ways do you wish the followers of Jesus had a stronger influence on our culture?**

There is certainly plenty of room for this!

4.   **How do followers of Jesus view our world differently than other people? What tension does this create?**

Encourage this kind of positive awareness of how others around us are gifted and blessed.

5.   **If followers of Jesus were "salt" and "light" in our world, how could that help to overcome the differences between them and those who don't follow Jesus?**

This could bring further emphasis to love as a powerful connection to others.

6.   **What convinces you that all human beings have great worth to God?**

Guide the discussion toward a higher awareness of God's amazing love for every individual. As you close, ask each person in the group to pray a sentence prayer that recognizes our dependence on God and his grace and truth.

Moving Forward

The goal here is to help group members grasp and be awed by their new identity and calling from Jesus to be salt and light in their daily environments.

Preparation for Session 5

Remember to point out the brief daily devotions that the group members can complete and which will help greatly in stimulating discussion in your next session. These devotions will enable everyone to dig into the Bible and start wrestling with the topics that will come up next time.

Session 5 — When Gracie Met Truthy

Bottom Line

In the life of Jesus and the love of Jesus, we see an incredible fullness of both grace and truth. The dynamics of this can lead to considerable tension for us, because we see Jesus being unpredictable and even inconsistent. It can seem so messy at times, so confusing. But that's the path we're to embrace as we follow Jesus in fully experiencing and extending both a fullness of grace and a fullness of truth.

Discussion Starter

Use the "Discussion Starter" printed in Session 5 of the Participant's Guide to "break the ice"—and to help everyone see the amazing complexity and unpredictability of Jesus in loving action.

Notes for Discussion Questions

1. **When you read the Bible (or hear it taught) and experience tension in your understanding of Jesus and how he lives and loves, is that tension something you try to resolve or are you comfortable with it?**

   Again, your genuine response will help open up everyone else in the group to share candidly.

2. **What's your understanding of the word "grace" and what it represents—both as coming from God and as conveyed by us to other people?**

    Encourage a God-centered focus that makes the most of his loving heart.

3. **What's is your understanding of the word "truth" and what it represents, both as coming from God and as conveyed by us to other people?**

    Bring attention to the biblical teachings that closely intertwine his truth and grace.

4. **What are the ways you recognize or experience tension between grace and truth? In which direction do you tend to lean?**

    Again, your honest response will help others open up.

5. **In what ways have you experienced both grace and truth?**

    Aim for clear-sighted recognition of how God has been at work in all your lives, and encourage gratitude for this.

6.   **Why is a "balance" between grace and truth the wrong way to think of what's being taught in this session? What is a better way to think of the relationship between grace and truth?**

Your goal here is to help everyone recognize how Jesus allowed the fullness of both grace and truth to guide his personal encounters with others—and we're to do the same. As you close, ask each person in the group to pray a sentence prayer that recognizes our dependence on God and his grace and truth.

Moving Forward

The goal here is to help everyone in the group recognize and embrace the tension involved in experiencing and extending the fullness of truth and the fullness of grace.

Preparation for Session 6

Remember to point out the brief daily devotions that the group members can complete and which will help greatly in stimulating discussion in your next session. These devotions will enable everyone to dig into the Bible and start wrestling with the topics that will come up next time.

Session 6 — Angry Birds

Bottom Line

God understands that the dynamics of grace and truth as evidenced in the life of Jesus—and as required in our lives as well—will bring a considerable amount of tension our way. But he wants us to grow increasingly more comfortable in living with that tension as we go forward on the pathway of love.

Discussion Starter

Use the "Discussion Starter" printed in Session 6 of the Participant's Guide to "break the ice"—and to help everyone come closer to sensing God's great desire to seek and to save the lost.

Notes for Discussion Questions

1. **In what ways do you sense alienation from God among people in your community?**

    Again, encourage the kind of sensitivity that helps everyone in your group recognize the need to take the gospel into your community.

2. **In what ways do you see evidence of self-righteousness among religious people in your community?**

    Openly recognize this grievous issue without voicing accusations directed against specific people.

3. **Are you convinced there's nothing you can do to cause God to love you more than he already does? Why or why not?**

    This can begin to open everyone's heart to a greater appreciation of the gospel.

4. **Are you convinced there's nothing *others* can do to cause God to love them more than he already does? Why or why not?**

    Encourage the kind of loving perspective that sees the gospel's full reach to each person, no matter how hopelessly lost in sin he or she seems to be.

5. **In what ways are you tempted to grow slack in your understanding and acceptance of God's *grace*?**

    Most of us need lots of help in becoming more honest with ourselves, so allow plenty of time for the discussion.

6.   **In what ways are you tempted to grow slack in your understand-**

      ing and acceptance of God's *truth*?

      Share your honest response here, encouraging everyone to do

      the same. As you close, ask each person in the group to pray a

      sentence prayer that recognizes our dependence on God and

      his grace and truth.

Moving Forward

The goal here is to help all group members encounter God's loving

heart in a fresh way that frees them to recognize the tragic lostness

of those trapped by sin and to fully rejoice when repentance and

restoration are achieved.

Preparation for Session 7

Remember to point out the brief daily devotions that the group mem-

bers can complete and which will help greatly in stimulating discus-

sion in your next session. These devotions will enable everyone to

dig into the Bible and start wrestling with the topics that will come

up next time.

Session 7 — Loopholes

Bottom Line

The followers of Jesus do not look for loopholes and shortcuts in their faith. Instead they align their hearts with the loving heart of God, and in every situation they ask this question: *What does love require of me?*

Discussion Starter

Use the "Discussion Starter" printed in Session 7 of the Participant's Guide to "break the ice"—and to help everyone see the danger and folly of looking for loopholes.

Notes for Discussion Questions

1.   **Why are we so eager to find loopholes—especially religious loopholes?**

     Let your honest answer lead the way for others.

2.   **How do Christians manufacture extra rules in order to preserve their own comforts or biases?**

     Again, the things you acknowledge and confess will help others in your group to do the same.

3. **How would you describe your view of theology? Do you see theology as helpful or harmful?**

    Help your group members recognize the deadness of doctrinal understanding void of genuine, loving service toward others.

4. **How can you tell if you're more in love with the commands in the Bible than with the *Commander*?**

    Help direct the discussion to the discussion points given in the DVD teaching content.

5. **Are you convinced that Jesus understood his Father's intentions as written in the Bible? Why or why not?**

    Encourage a strong focus on Christ and his relationship as the beloved Son of his heavenly Father. You may want to explore passages such as Matthew 3:17; 17:5; Luke 10:22; John 3:35; 5:20; 12:45–47; 15:15; and 17:26.

6.   **How would you answer the question: "What does love re-
     quire of me?"**

     The goal here is to help everyone in the group build the habit

     into their lives of regularly asking, "What does love require of

     me?" As you close, ask each person in the group to pray a

     sentence prayer that recognizes our dependence on God and

     his grace and truth.

Moving Forward

The goal here is to help everyone in the group accept and embrace

our ongoing obligation to extend love to others in the name of Je-

sus as the true fulfillment of what Scripture requires.

Preparation for Session 8

Remember to point out the brief daily devotions that the group

members can complete and which will help greatly in stimulating

discussion in your next session. These devotions will enable every-

one to dig into the Bible and start wrestling with the topics that will

come up next time.

Session 8 — Working It Out

Bottom Line

Our obligation to love others, and our privilege of having a loving influence on others, will mean that we need to refrain from anything that hurts us, from anything that hurts others, and from anything that masters us. Then we're free to fully engage in our calling of love.

Discussion Starter

Use the "Discussion Starter" printed in Session 8 of the Participant's Guide to "break the ice"—and to help everyone see the great opportunity for influence that is ours simply by loving others.

Notes for Discussion Questions

1. **How central is *love for God* and *love for others* to your understanding of the Bible's message?**

   The goal here is to help intensify each one's personal recognition of the supreme importance of love.

2.   **How central is *love for God* and *love for others* to the moral and ethical standards you apply to your life?**

Allow plenty of time for the discussion, to encourage honest recognition of where we need help in this regard.

3.   **How have you already grown in understanding what *love* requires? How have your attitudes changed over time?**

This could lead to strong affirmations of what God has been doing in expanding everyone's heart.

4.   **What part do our beliefs play in the influence we have on other people?**

Your discussion may lead to the foundational role that our *true* beliefs play in determining our behavior.

5.   **What challenges are you likely to encounter if you truly seek to avoid hurting yourself, hurting others, and being mastered by anything?**

Remember again, your genuine response will help everyone else in the group open up to share candidly. As you close, ask each person in the group to pray a sentence prayer that recognizes our dependence on God and his grace and truth.

Moving Forward

The goal here is to help group members conclude this series with a strengthened habit of examining and pursuing their daily lives through the filter of loving God and loving others.

Zondervan Small Group Bible Study YouTube Playlist

Watch Over 100 Full Bible Study Sessions for Free

Watch the entire first lesson for many of Zondervan's DVD based Bible studies. No more guessing on the content, instead you get the full video experience by being able to see and evaluate the complete first lesson of each multi-lesson Bible study.

Each video is easy to share with your friends, small group or Bible study. Just hit the "share" button under the video and send it via email, Facebook, or Twitter.

Watch Bible study sessions from bestselling authors like Andy Stanley, Timothy Keller, Anne Graham Lotz, Bill Hybels, Craig Groeschel, Jim Cymbala, John Ortberg, Lysa TerKeurst, and many more.

Zondervan video-based group Bible studies are available on DVD, and many are available for download. These video Bible studies feature a variety of topics from many authors, and are available wherever small group resources and curriculum are sold.

Watch sessions from bestselling studies including:

* *Guardrails* by Andy Stanley
* *The Reason for God* by Timothy Keller
* *The Christian Atheist* by Craig Groeschel
* *Undaunted* by Christine Caine
* *The Circle Maker* by Mark Batterson

www.Zondervan.com/BibleStudy

ZONDERVAN®
.com

The New Rules for Love, Sex, and Dating: A DVD Study

Andy Stanley

"Are you who the person you are looking for is looking for?"

Single? Looking for the "right person"? Thinking that if you met the "right person" everything would turn out "right"?

Think again.

In *The New Rules for Love, Sex, and Dating*, Andy Stanley explores the challenges, assumptions, and land mines associated with dating in the twenty-first century. Best of all, he offers the most practical and uncensored advice you will ever hear on this topic.

Not for the faint of heart, *The New Rules for Love, Sex, and Dating* challenges single Christ followers to step up and set a new standard for this generation!

The *New Rules for Love, Sex, and Dating*:

- Unveils what God says that will lead to success in dating and marriage,
- Transforms the way guys think about women,
- Reveals common myths about sex outside of marriage,
- Prepares men and women to one day say "I do" and mean it,
- And much more.

"If you don't want a marriage like the majority of marriages, then stop dating like the majority of daters!"

—Andy Stanley

Available in stores and online!

Guardrails

Avoiding Regrets in Your Life

Andy Stanley

[Guardrails: a system designed to keep vehicles from straying into dangerous or off-limit areas.]

They're everywhere, but they don't really get much attention . . . until somebody hits one. And then, more often than not, it is a lifesaver.

Ever wonder what it would be like to have guardrails in other areas of your life—areas where culture baits you to the edge of disaster and then chastises you when you step across the line?

Your friendships. Your finances. Your marriage. Maybe your greatest regret could have been avoided if you had established guardrails.

In this six-session video based study, Andy Stanley challenges us to stop flirting with disaster and establish some personal guardrails.

Session titles:
1. Direct and Protect
2. Why Can't We Be Friends?
3. Flee Baby Flee!
4. Me and the Mrs.
5. The Consumption Assumption
6. Once and For All

Available in stores and online!

Taking Responsibility for Your Life

Because Nobody Else Will

Andy Stanley

RESPONSIBILITIES.

We all have them. But we don't all take them as seriously as we ought to. Wouldn't it be great, though, if we all took responsibility for the things we are responsible for? Wouldn't it be great if you took responsibility for everything you're responsible for? It's time to stop the finger-pointing and excuse-making and to remove the "ir" in irresponsible.

In this 4-part study, Andy Stanley tells us it's time to ask ourselves, "Am I REALLY taking responsibility for my life?"

Session titles:
1. Let the Blames Begin
2. The Disproportionate Life
3. This Is No Time to Pray
4. Embracing Your Response Ability

Designed for use with the *Taking Responsibility for Your Life Participant's Guide.*

Available in stores and online!

Staying in Love

Falling in Love Is Easy, Staying in Love Requires a Plan

Andy Stanley

We all know what's required to fall in love…a pulse. Falling in love is easy. But staying there—that's something else entirely. With more than a thousand matchmaking services available today and new ones springing up all the time, finding a romantic match can be easier than ever. But staying together with the one you've found seems to be the real challenge.

So, is it possible for two people to fall in love and actually stay there? Absolutely! Let pastor and author Andy Stanley show you how in this four-session, video-based study that also features a separate participant's guide.

Session titles include:
1. The Juno Dilemma
2. Re-Modeling
3. Feelin' It
4. Multiple Choice Marriage

Your Move

Four Questions to Ask When You Don't Know What to Do

Andy Stanley

We are all faced with decisions that we never anticipated having to make. And, we usually have to make them quickly. In this four session video group study, author and pastor Andy Stanley discusses four questions that will help participants make sound decisions with God's help. Follow Andy as he teaches how every decision and its outcomes become a permanent part of your story, what to do when you feel the need to pause before taking action, and how to make more of this life by making sound decisions.

The DVD-ROM and separate participant's guide contain everything you need to create your group experience:

Available in stores and online!

Starting Point
Starter Kit

Find Your Place
in the Story

Andy Stanley and the
Starting Point Team

Starting Point is an exploration of God's grand story and where you fit into the narrative. This proven, small group experience is carefully designed to meet the needs of

- Seekers that are curious about Christianity
- Starters that are new to a relationship with Jesus
- Returners that have been away from church for a while

Starting Point is an accepting, conversational environment where people learn about God's story and their places in it. Starting Point helps participants explore the Bible and begin to understand key truths of the Christian faith.

Carefully refined to enhance community, the ten interactive sessions in Starting Point encourage honest exploration. The *Conversation Guide*, which includes a five-disk audio series featuring Andy Stanley, helps each participant enjoy and engage fully with the small group experience.

About This Starter Kit

The *Starting Point Starter Kit* is geared for ministry leaders. It consists of the following:

- Four-color *Starting Point Conversation Guide* containing five audio disks, with over five hours of teaching by Andy Stanley
- *Starter Guide* providing step-by-step instructions on how to successfully launch and sustain the Starting Point ministry
- A Starting Point TNIV Bible
- One-hour leader training DVD
- Interactive CD containing promotional videos, pre-service marketing graphics, leader training tools, and administrative resources

Available in stores and online!

Share Your Thoughts

With the Author: Your comments will be forwarded to the author when you send them to *zauthor@zondervan.com*.

With Zondervan: Submit your review of this book by writing to *zreview@zondervan.com*.

Free Online Resources at
www.zondervan.com

Zondervan AuthorTracker: Be notified whenever your favorite authors publish new books, go on tour, or post an update about what's happening in their lives at www.zondervan.com/authortracker.

Daily Bible Verses and Devotions: Enrich your life with daily Bible verses or devotions that help you start every morning focused on God. Visit www.zondervan.com/newsletters.

Free Email Publications: Sign up for newsletters on Christian living, academic resources, church ministry, fiction, children's resources, and more. Visit www.zondervan.com/newsletters.

Zondervan Bible Search: Find and compare Bible passages in a variety of translations at www.zondervanbiblesearch.com.

Other Benefits: Register yourself to receive online benefits like coupons and special offers, or to participate in research.

■ ZONDERVAN®

ZONDERVAN.com/
AUTHORTRACKER
follow your favorite authors